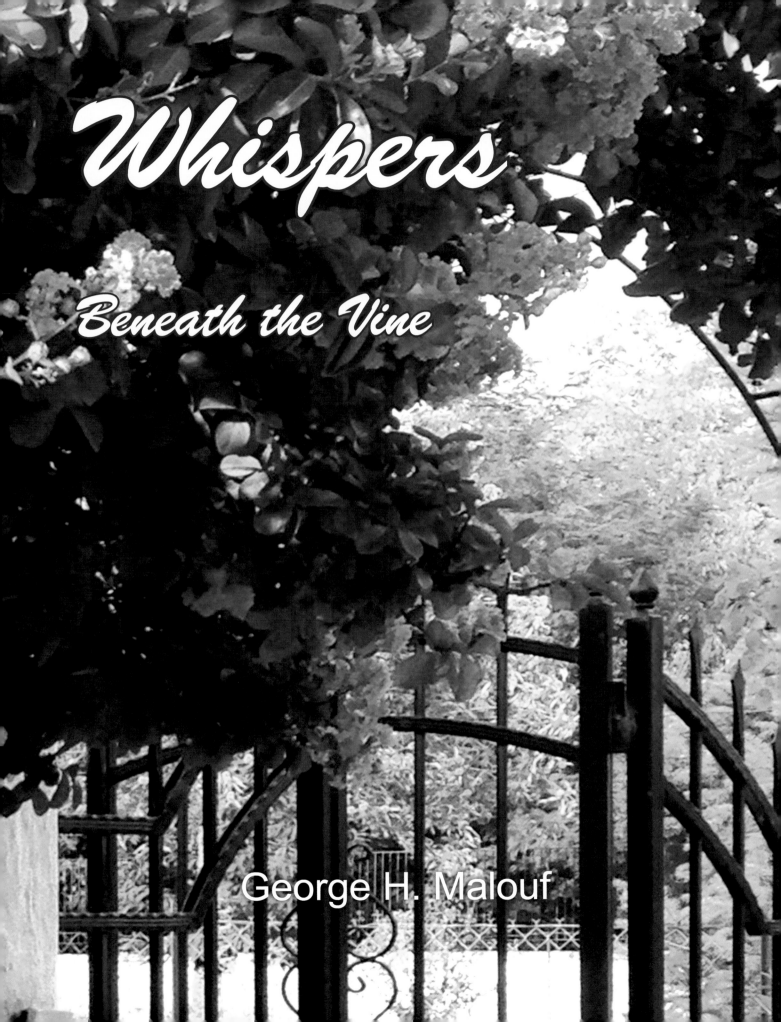

Print information available on the last page

Rev. date: 05/17/2018

To order additional copies of this book, contact:
Xlibris
1-888-795-4274
www.Xlibris.com
Orders@Xlibris.com

Whispers
Beneath the Vine

George H. Malouf

Foreward

My constant attempts at producing a work of poetry, though laborious as it may seem, is a source of solace and satisfaction for me; it tends to carry me into that special, magical dimension, which is devoid of boredom and depression of spirit.

Somehow, I seem to find myself in a kind of "Elysium," with a euphoric state, where I begin to jot down my feelings and observations, as I reminisce over those golden moments of love, and the everpresent divinity that are present in the surrounding natural beauty. I find myself in a sort of magnitizing mood that brings me closer to the forgotten reality.

As a poet, I try to render each floating stanza, of my somewhat unorthodox style, on a fabulous panoramic canvas, for all to behold. In doing so, I hope to bring some inspiration to those who read it. In my aspirations to reach the heights of expression, I try to establish some rhythmic cadence, without having to sacrifice that certain spontaneity in my feelings and thought.

To my beloved Yiota:

....

There, in the deepest niche of my heart;
At the epi-center of where true love thrives,
I find you dwelling, forever.

Contents

O' Life

O' life,
Let me cleanse
My eyes
With the glow
Of your beauty.

Allow me
To live
A moment,
In the keeping
Of your precious eyes.

Imprison me,
Forever,
Confined
Within the deepest niche
Of your heart,

That I may feel
Your every
Heart-beat;
And inhale
Your every precious breath.

Let my spirit intermingle
With yours
That we may,
Together,
Roam the limits, unconfined-

Unbothered to reach
The heights of elation;
Intoxicated
By the fumes
Of our yearning love.

Behold, O Muse

Behold, O Muse, that torch of freedom,
Eternally burning- ever so bright,

As yon, tall graceful-queen stands vigil
With her symbols of Liberty, fathoms in height;

And her beacon, planted, on her door steps-
Ever so deep, with toil,

Continues to stir the millions
To seek her sacred soil.

Tonight

Tonight, a thousand guests
Will visit, by my side...
The moon, the stars,
And my memories of you.

Like treasures
From the distant past,
The memoirs will come,
One-by-one.

Then, the sojourn sky
Will shed a thousand tears,
As I call out your name,
In silence, once and again.

I will try to hold you, forever,
In my wakeful heart;
And keep you
In my warm embrace.

Then, when the curtains of night
Begin to lift,
With the first rays
Of dawn,

I'll behold
Your ambrosial beauty
As it rises, gracefully,
On my flank—

Bringing radiant glory
To the blanketing darkness;
And piercing the very heart
Of the nocturnal shade.

I saw

I saw
The first farm-house lights
Flickering
In the distance,

As farm boys started to grapple
For their clothes,
To begin
Their daily chores.

In the lingering shadows
Of darkness,
I heard troops of geese,
Anxious for their expected departure-

Setting, in motion,
Their early flights
To search for their fields
Of feast and refuge…

Far from the stinging reach
Of man's killing sticks,
And the thousand and one beacons
Of the city.

I saw my own words
As they gushed forth
In the eye of night,
In ordered succession-

Lining up,
In formation,
Like soldiers on the field
Of thought-

Ignoring
The soft comfort
Of the heavy mantle
Of dear sleep.

The Solemn Maiden

Once, an aura of beauty enveloped
The silken softness of her skin-

Filling her face with angelic symmetry
And life's warm glow;

And the ever present shimmer, in her eyes,
Would whisper softly of secret things-

From behind her veiled beauty;
And her permissive, long eyelashes.

Her lips would speak...
Yet, they did not seem to move.

Now, after the incident, with the fiery onset,
Her God-bestowed features were gone, forever-

Replaced, by the decrepitude,
In the hideous masks of demons.

Her facial symmetry and alluring glow
Were now, forever, lifted;

And the shine, in her eyes-
Replaced by unhampered tears.

Her lips, a mangled heap,
Were, now, speechless and silent-

As she pranced about, moving,
From one dark niche to another,

Attempting to avoid the piercing stares
Of those, who would look her way

The Golden Sand

As the sun began to shed its golden crown;
And the serene, evening air began to fill
With the melodies of that sacred heart song;
And the camp fire became clad with the glow
of a thousand and one sparkles of light-

We saw the golden sand, at rest
Beneath the shifting cover of the restless sea,
Starting to melt away, with the approaching dark;
And the great waters beginning to unleash their fury
Upon the once silent shore.

For a sojourn moment, we beheld the moon,
Clad in its silvery light,
Shining with brilliance and radiance;
And climbing above us, upward, askance-
As if riding weightless upon the wind.

Like a swift raven, it rose up,
Circling in the foyers of heaven-
To rule over the untamed sky,
With its glimmering myriad of stars,
And the shimmer of divine grace.

And when, at last, our eyes did meet,
I began to perceive the springs of meadows
In her fallen tears;
And, for the first time, I heard her calling-
As my heart began to plummet…falling, falling,

Till the heavens, in sweet embrace,
Ensnared the early light of dawn;
And the glorious sun kissed, softly, her face-
Showering her spirit with grace and beauty,
Like the soft breeze at early morn.

Land Of Promise

Nations sought salvation and refuge
Within her tall, impregnable gates;

And the masses clampered to her open arms,
Fleeing the fury of potentates.

One by one, the anxious pilgrims came,
Her hostile wilderness, to brave and tame;

And to Replace suppression with promise,
Within her growing fame.

They embarked on her colonization
With chant and praise;

And endured all hardships
And detrimental malaise.

Their blood, their tears, was the price they spent
For true liberty and equality's sake.

They harnassed each opportunity,
Their livelyhood, to make;

And reaped justice, with their mind unbent,
To sew morality within her midst.

At last, their loved ones would find peace,
With their cries for freedom and power to resist;

And, in prayer and hope,
They would continue the search to find

The sure way to success,
And their ease of mind.

The Lonely Old Man

The lonely old-man, often repeated
That "no one knew what the moment held,
Nor what the new morn might bring."

Often, he watched the moments turn to hours;
When the veils of mist would be lifted
From the face of earth;

And small birds would begin their ascent-
To ride upon the shoulders of the breeze-
Busily, going to and fro.

He would watch the angry winds,
Swishing by the frightened bush;
And recollect his yesterdays-

When his love affair of a lifetime
Became nothing more
Than a small whisper in the wind.

He would remember the angry storm
That came, by stealth,
To sever the rose from the stalk.

For him, it was a moment when,
like the "thief in the night,"
She vanished-whisked away into eternity.

She was gone-like the obscurity of the night;
The dew on the blades of grass;
And the flower's tear, at early dawn.

Soon, he thought,
The fresh ethereal-winds would return
To give him new life and rejuvenation;

And the radiant sunshine would fall upon him
To warm his old, aching bones;
And he would tarry, unbothered, beyond reach.

The Treasures In The Mind

A wise owl, once, said:

"The mind is precious for its vast stores
Of knowledge and information;

And it is vital for the very existence
Of all God's creatures."

"As a lighted beacon, with its rays of hope,
It pierces the stormy night,

To guide the strayed vessels home-
Away from the ominous ways of desolation."

"The mind steers each creature adrift-
Away from the perils of uncertainty;

And, without its illumination,
One could risk facing dangers, unaware."

My Little Imaginary Boat

My little, imaginary boat sailed gently-
Down the winding river's course.

It was swept with the rushing torrents,
As they barreled their way,

Above the insignificant pebbles,
In the sand below.

For a short span, my vessel lingered,
Dallying by the banks of the rushing stream,

Until, it arrived at a distant bend-
Beyond yon hillock and its carpets green

Like the isolated foam of the pummeling sea,
It seemed to disappear, with each ebb and flow,

To disembark, at some distant shore-
Carrying its message of love and Peace.

I Find Me Roaming

I find me roaming the vast firmament,
In search of my "evening star,"

Guided by yon bright, crescent beacon,
To alight, safely, on your shores.

...I will look for your beckoning abode,
In the midst of myriads of blossoms,

That embelish your inviting
Carpets of green;

And find me strown
In your fragrant paradise-

Beholden to your angelic vision
...Oh, so fair!

If, only, I were a true artisan,
I would embroider your beautiful sight,

With the purest threads of gold,
Upon each of the plethoral pages of eternity!

I Felt The Crispness

I felt the crispness of the pre-dawn air,
As it nibbled away, slowly,

At my nose and ears-
Kissing, repeatedly, my cheeks and face.

And, as I sat alone,
I gazed upon the face of God;

And pondered over
The deepest space of night-

Suddenly, I was awakened, by the fresh,
Crackling kisses of the pre-dawn air-

In time to see the country lake,
Beginning to mirror

The first golden rays of the sun,
peaking over the distant horizon.

I watched, in wonder, as the shimmering sparkle
Of the numerous stars of night

Began to disappear,
Behind the brightening veil of day.

I saw the clouds, dipping gently,
Before the waking meadow-

To kiss, softly, the dry face of earth,
With their incessant falling-tears.

The Earth Is Aging

The meadow gasped-on
"Mother earth was aging;

Parasites continued to linger
In the folds of her hems."

It continued to languish,
With the re-occuring thought,

That the most life-threatening parasite of all,
With its ever mounting destruction-

To lay waste the very foundation
Of its own abode-

Was none other
Than the brute, called "man."

When I Awakened

When I awakened, in the midst of night,
I felt your warm body;

And saw your glowing face-
Rising on my flank,

Bringing glory to my being;
And spearing the heart of the nocturnal shade.

I began to perceive the imprint of my soul
On the turning pages of my life,

As it was swept, by the gentle currents,
Beneath my spirit in flight.

For you have, truly, captured my soul;
And loosened the reins of my essence.

You have imprisoned my eyesight;
And influenced my soaring heart.

And your graceful body-
Like the swan of the lake-

Glided into the castle of my dreams;
And found me speechless, with wonder-

Awaiting to do the biddings
Of my rejuvenated heart's demands.

A Muse, With Unbridled Imagination

A muse, with unbridled imagination,
Once declared that:

He had seen an empty space
As wide as a multitude of universes-

In the midst of the huge void
Of non-existence...to a man yet unborn;

And during a span of time,
Not yet felt by life,

He beheld time-the river of life,
In its occupation of space,

Flowing hurriedly
To reach the outstretched arms

Of its mother-
The "Sea of Eternity."

He felt the hand of the Lord moving therein,
Shaking the banks of the river-

Loosening the grains of sand from the shorelines;
And hewing them into small life forms.

In The Oasis of My Dreams

O Damsel of my dreams-
To grace so sincere-

Approach me, dearest
Come close; come near.

Travel with me to yon "oasis,"
That fertile valley of my dreams!

For, in the heart of night,
I find me awake, haunted by love's passion.

Like the raging tempest, o'er the mighty sea-
Bellowing away in a horrid fashion.

And, in the late hour of every eve,
I seem to lose my power- escape, to achieve.

I find me returning, to my chamber of sleep,
To continue the quarrel-that wounds me deep.

...They say that "the price of a true love
Can never be cheap-

Like the unscaleable heights
Of the mountain-e'er so steep."

...I find myself propelled,
My destiny, to achieve-

...So many obstacles, in my path,
I must conquer and leave.

For, at the heart of the rose,
The enticing nectar is born-

That attracts the humming bird
In the early morn.

The Ancients

The ancients perceived man
As a helpless grain of sand in the hourglass-

Plummeting, without recourse, or recompense-
Seemingly lost-beyond reach and comfort,

As he continues to eulogize the past-
Ignoring the glorification of the present;

And failing to embrace the future
With open arms.

The Earth Applauded

The earth applauded
Among the tree branches of the field,

As the white tufts of heaven
Continued to sail away,

In the vastness
Of the air, above us.

...We saw the scurrying streams, gushing forth,
From the Springs of Planiterou;

And the flowing waters, rushing by-
Nibling away at our naked feet;

And covering the insignificant pebbles,
Below the mirrored surface-

Without notice
Of our sweet embrace.

...We dreamed of sailing away, forever,
Upon the thousand and one rivulets,

As they disappeared
Beyond the distant hills;

And found ourselves,
Graced by a melodious muse-

Riding upon that magic tapestry
Of incessant, joyful dreams-

Rising above the great summits
Of Mt. Helmos.

The Beginning And The End

The savant declared that:

"There is a beginning to every end;
And an end to every beginning."

"For, we are like the seeds of a tree,
Scattered about

By the winds of circumstance-
Falling into the rivers of the spring."

"We wind our way to our mother, the sea-
Inseparable from our source."

"We are like the lashing waves of the sea,
Ebbing and flowing to distant shores."

"We rise and fall
Like the clouds of heaven."

"At times, we are like the golden sand, at rest,
Beneath the shifting cover of the meandering sea."

I Heard My Motherland

I heard my motherland sobbing of pain,
In the midst of darkness.

I saw her crying, during the day,
Trying to reach out to the Benevolent One.

I witnessed her, weeping of sorrow,
In the silence of the night-

Struggling to catch her breath,
As she coughed out her very own lifeblood.

I Love You

I love you, because
You are the essence-

The very source of joy
In my life.

Each time, that I see you,
I behold the dawning of a new day,

With all its beauty
And all its splendour;

And I witness the rising sun,
In all its glory,

As it reaches above the head
Of Mount Helmos, aloft.

I see the sparkling waters,
Of Planitero Springs-

Running, ever so pure
And clear;

And the flowers
Of the meadow,

That invade the flanks
Of the rushing river,

With their bright colors
And intoxicating smell.

When The Day Broke

When the day broke,
In all its beauty,

And the glorious sun rose
O'er the heads of the lofty hills,

I witnessed the stream,
Running clear & bright;

And the flowers,
So fair to scent and sight.

I beheld the swelling sea
With its lashing waves;

And the residual froth,
Frolicking, among the rocks—

Scattering away;
And disappearing, suddenly,

In their flank,
With the sparkling mist.

In Woolen Tents

In woolen tents-low and black-
Abides the Bedouin with his eager pack.

He Surrounds himself with his countless herd
Of gloaming sheep, and black spotted goats.

He tends, with the "Jinn",
To his black-mained steeds;

And his humped-back friends-
The bellowing camels.

He continues to span the desert,
With the greatest of ease-

From beyond the date palms,
And the shelter of green oasis,

To the night time whispers
Of a cooling breeze.

He lives in his palace,
Of sheep-skin hair,

Like a sheikh, in majesty,
With his outspread skirts,

Resembling the hillocks
On the distant plains.

The Murmuring Brook

The cedar tree overheard
The murmuring brook,

In its chatter
With the spring,

Remarking that:
"The insignificant man

Thinks that the universe
Belongs to him and to his kind."

"...Does he not realize that
The universe was here

Long, before he came
Into being;

And that it will continue
To be here-

Long, after
He has passed?"

In The Deepest Niche

There, in the deepest niche of my heart-
There, where true love, eternally, thrives-

I find you dwelling forever.
...Yet, I continue to call out your name

More than a thousand times, in an instant-
To share the night, in my beckoning embrace.

The Ceaseless Chattering

The ceaseless chattering, of the brook,
Continues to repeat the story of life,

To the ever stretching trees-
With their chlorophylous laurels-

With every fleeting drop
Of its precious water,

...And the birds, of heaven, continue to glide
Through the morning air,

Attempting to reach that green oasis-
Their refuge, for life's living elixir,

In those pure droplets-
Heaven's tears.

That Far Echoing Bellow

That far echoing bellow
Of a hee-hawing donkey-

Ever, so rebellious, and stubborn,
As he yanks away at his enslaving shackles;

And the distant crowing of an anxious rooster-
Announcing breakfast time, for his masters to hear,

Are a small part of the beauty of nature,
And God's gift to all.

Nightly

Nightly,
I lay me
Down to sleep,

In the tender,
Tender keeping
Of your sweet embrace;

Only to find out, as I awaken
My tear-laden pillow,
Occupying your proche, intimate space.

The Symphony of Life

The symphony of life continues
With the sound
Of yon cascading waterfall
As it empties its wares,
In the pooling of the meadow;

And, in the distance, the sounds
Of a parading rooster,
Continue to bellow,
As he keeps an account
Of his harem's roster-

Readying to deal
A mighty blow,
Upon those,
Who dare to approach
The bounds of his vigilance.

Like a sovereign, on his throne,
He carries his pride
with an adamant stance,
And absence of fear,
To subjugate without lenience.

America Is My Country

America is my country; America is my home.
She is my refuge-my great freedom's dome.

She is my salvation and solace-
A mighty citadel against all foes.

For she is an impregnable fort
Against all storms and woes.

America, the beautiful, shall always be
The beacon of freedom and the land of liberty.

America is my country; America is my home.
She is my refuge-my great freedom's dome

For You, My Child

For you, my child, on your wedding day,
I borrowed this moment to try to say;

And let me say it, clear and loud:
That you've made us happy and very proud!

For you, my child, I wish to pray
For God to guide you, each and every day;

May your mind be worry clear-
That you'll have, only God, to fear;

That your life be trouble free-
Filling your heart with joyful glee;

And may your love, for each other-
That here does show-

Continue, along the way,
To grow and grow.

...And as you reach each milestone,
Along the way,

Remember these words,
As you live each day:

"To regret, I shall owe no moment;
To contentment, I shall owe a few."

...And, in a lasting, resounding word,
May the blessings of our Lord;

And the pure love
That brought you together,

Continue to bind you
Forever and ever.

With My Spirit

With my spirit, in flight,
I looked down from the astral heaven-

With all its shimmer and vast expanse;
And beheld the village lights spilling down,

Unto the lap of Mt. Helmos and the valleys beyond.
...Shortly, I witnessed the early morning sun,

Peaking over yon distant horizon-
Lifting the cover of darkness from the waking earth.

I saw flashes of lightening;
And heard the thundering echoes

Of distant drum beats, resounding in the air-
Signaling the readiness of anxious troops.

I began to sense the hastening moment
For the upcoming battle,

Over the eminent dominance
Of yon darkening sky.

I beheld cascading waterfalls,
Ceaselessly storing;

And churning heaven's tears,
In agitated pools, down below.

I heard the constant song of the rivulet,
Winding its way along a familiar path-

Beyond the reach of the nearby hills;
And the plush carpet of green and yellow-

Soothing its rugged flanks,
Along its wayward passage to the sea.

Look Away, My Child

Look away, my child, as I begin to fade;
And remember me in my wakeful state.

For now, I begin to shed that earthly garment,
Without despair and signs of lament.

Like a centaur, galloping away, embracing fear,
I find me trying to evade yon Amazon's spear.

For I must embrace that final glory,
Reliving each moment of our life's story;

And seek out those caryatids, of ancient times,
To hear those melodious harp-string rhymes;

And relive the goodness of that fleeing instance,
Where we, together, shared our short existance.

...I must endear that wondrous hour,
Until it resonates with joyful power.

For love and peace reside there, forever-
Beyond the boundaries of forever and ever.

...And, now, I'll keep a smile on my face;
And meet the heavens in sweet embrace.

For, only there, will our lives never end-
Like the tarrying whisper in the wind.

Beginnings And Endings

The murmuring brook,
In its constant chatter,
Remarked that: "beginnings and endings
Are the cycles of existance."

That: "amidst the plethora of beginnings,
Ours came into being,
When the hands of the Lord
Stirred the waters in the pool of essence."

It remarked that: "it was long,
Before the ages of ages,
That a tiny bubble burst into the void
And the vastness of eternity;

And that it was that instant,
When our universal dimension
Began to inhale and exhale,
Bringing life unto the essence of being."

"It was, also, at that time,
That life began to emerge
In all its forms, and all its colors;
In all its setbacks, and all its triumphs,

Expanding freely
Into the emptiness,
Unfettered -
Without bounds."

Within The Mind Of The Poet

The ripples in the water,
Mirroring the blue heaven up above;

The desert's mysteries
That consume the mind of the Bedouin;

The ethereal chanting, of angelic hosts,
Heralding, with grace, the Divinity around us;

The harmonious cadence of virtue
That quivers the very strings of our soul;

The muse descending, from the heights of elation,
To sway us into a nostalgic state;

The sirens cradled among the boulders,
As the waves race to drench the sandy beach;

The sonorous splendour, without bounds,
Of the unchained stormy sea;

The words, lining up choreographically,
To begin the rhythmic dances before our eyes

...All this is, but the spring board,
Within the mind of the poet!

Printed in the United States
By Bookmasters